Lerner SPORTS

ALL-STAR SMACKDOWN

CAITLIN CLARK VS. CHERYL MILLER

WHO WOULD WIN?

SARAH ROGGIO

Lerner Publications ◆ Minneapolis

To my hometown librarians, for nurturing my love of reading

Lerner Publications Company
An imprint of Lerner Publishing Group, Inc.
241 First Avenue North
Minneapolis, MN 55401 USA

For reading levels and more information, look up this title at www.lernerbooks.com.

Main body text set in Aptifer Sans LT Pro. Typeface provided by Linotype AG.

Editor: Anne E. Hill

Library of Congress Cataloging-in-Publication Data

Names: Roggio, Sarah, author.
Title: Caitlin Clark vs. Cheryl Miller : who would win? / Sarah Roggio.
Other titles: Caitlin Clark versus Cheryl Miller
Description: Minneapolis, MN : Lerner Publications, [2026] | Series: All-star smackdown (Lerner sports) | Includes bibliographical references and index. | Audience: Ages 7–11 | Audience: Grades 2–3 | Summary: "Cheryl Miller is a women's basketball legend, and Caitlin Clark is taking the game to new levels of skill and popularity. Can you decide which player is better? Explore their careers and pick a winner"— Provided by publisher.
Identifiers: LCCN 2024038766 (print) | LCCN 2024038767 (ebook) | ISBN 9798765668504 (library binding) | ISBN 9798765683439 (paperback) | ISBN 9798765675939 (epub)
Subjects: LCSH: Clark, Caitlin, 2002-—Biography—Juvenile literature. | Miller, Cheryl, 1964-—Biography—Juvenile literature. | Women basketball players—United States—Statistics—Juvenile literature. | Women basketball players—United States—Biography—Juvenile literature.
Classification: LCC GV884.C554 R64 2026 (print) | LCC GV884.C554 (ebook) | DDC 796.323092 [B]—dc23/eng/20240909

LC record available at https://lccn.loc.gov/2024038766
LC ebook record available at https://lccn.loc.gov/2024038767

Manufactured in the United States of America
1-1011544-53818-10/22/2024

TABLE OF CONTENTS

Cheryl Miller

INTRODUCTION

SHARPSHOOTERS

Cheryl Miller and Caitlin Clark are known as basketball sharpshooters. Both are famous for sinking game-changing shots for their teams. They have also changed the game of women's basketball.

- Cheryl Miller set a California record of 105 points in a high school game.
- Miller led the University of Southern California (USC) to two NCAA titles in a row.
- Caitlin Clark set an NCAA record by scoring 3,951 career points at the University of Iowa.
- Clark was the first overall pick in the 2024 Women's National Basketball Association (WNBA) draft.

In 1982, Cheryl Miller was playing for Riverside Polytechnic High School in California. Her team faced rival Norte Vista High School. Cheryl wanted to beat her record of 77 points in one game. She had set this record in 1981 against Norte Vista.

As a forward, Cheryl knew how to score close to the basket. She also needed to make her long shots. She hit her first six jump shots of the game. Soon, she had scored 78 points to break her own record. But Cheryl kept playing until she set a new California state school record for girls. She racked up 105 points in the game! Riverside beat Norte Vista.

Caitlin Clark

Forty-two years later, Caitlin Clark also broke a big record. In February 2024, Clark was playing for the University of Iowa Hawkeyes. Her team faced the University of Michigan Wolverines. Clark wanted to break an NCAA Division I basketball scoring record. She only needed eight points to top 3,527, the most points ever scored in a women's college basketball career in the US.

Point guards such as Clark must be able to dribble, pass, and shoot the ball. Clark scored Iowa's first five points of the game. Then she planted her feet near the Hawkeyes' image on the center of the court.

She was setting up the long three-point shot that made her famous. *Swish!* She sank the basket to break the scoring record! She finished her senior season by breaking the men's basketball scoring record as well. Her 3,951 points will be hard to beat.

Both Miller and Clark are big names in women's basketball. But who would win if they played against each other? Compare their stats and achievements to make the call!

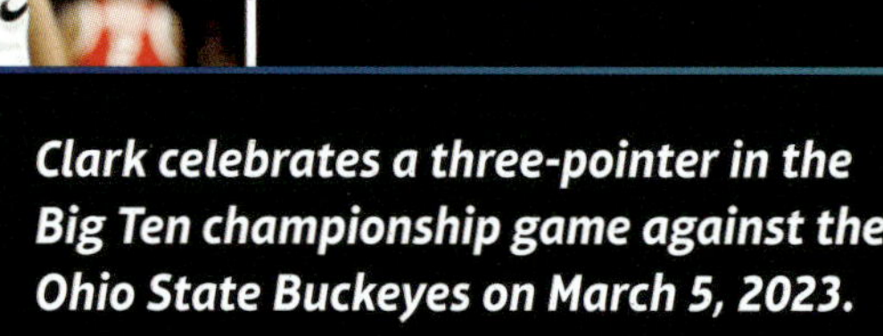

Clark celebrates a three-pointer in the Big Ten championship game against the Ohio State Buckeyes on March 5, 2023.

Clark gets past an Ohio State defender in January 2024.

CHAPTER 1

Miller takes a shot against the University of Tennessee in March 1984.

BORN BALLERS

Cheryl Miller and Caitlin Clark were both raised in athletic families. Cheryl was born on January 3, 1964, in Riverside, California. Her younger brother, Reggie Miller, was also a basketball player. As an adult, he played for the National Basketball Association's (NBA) Indiana Pacers. As kids, Cheryl always won when she played Reggie one-on-one.

In high school, Reggie scored 40 points in one game. Then he learned Cheryl scored her record 105 points that same night. Cheryl led her high school team to four state championships. Over two hundred colleges wanted Cheryl to play for them.

Cheryl Miller (middle) and brother Reggie Miller (right) in September 2012

She chose USC. Miller graduated from USC in 1986. She wanted to continue her career after college. But at the age of 22, Miller injured her knee and had to stop playing. Her brother still says she may be the greatest US women's basketball player in history.

Miller (middle) with USC teammates Paula McGee (left) and Pamela McGee (right) after their 1984 NCAA championship win

Caitlin Clark trying out for the 2018 USA Basketball Women's World Cup Team

Caitlin Clark was born on January 22, 2002, in Des Moines, Iowa. She was also from a basketball-loving family. Her father and uncle both played college basketball. Caitlin could dribble at the age of five. By sixth grade, she was known for her passes and three-point shots.

As a teen, Caitlin (left) played for the All Iowa Attack team.

Caitlin played point guard for Dowling Catholic High School. In one game, she scored 60 points. She chose to play for the University of Iowa Hawkeyes. In her first year, Clark set a new women's basketball record at the school with 799 points and 214 assists.

CONSIDER THIS

Caitlin Clark was athletic as a child. She played basketball, soccer, volleyball, softball, tennis, and golf. But in high school, she decided she was best at basketball.

By her last year at Iowa, Clark was a star. She held many more records. Clark graduated and entered the 2024 WNBA draft. The Indiana Fever chose her with the first pick in the first round of the draft.

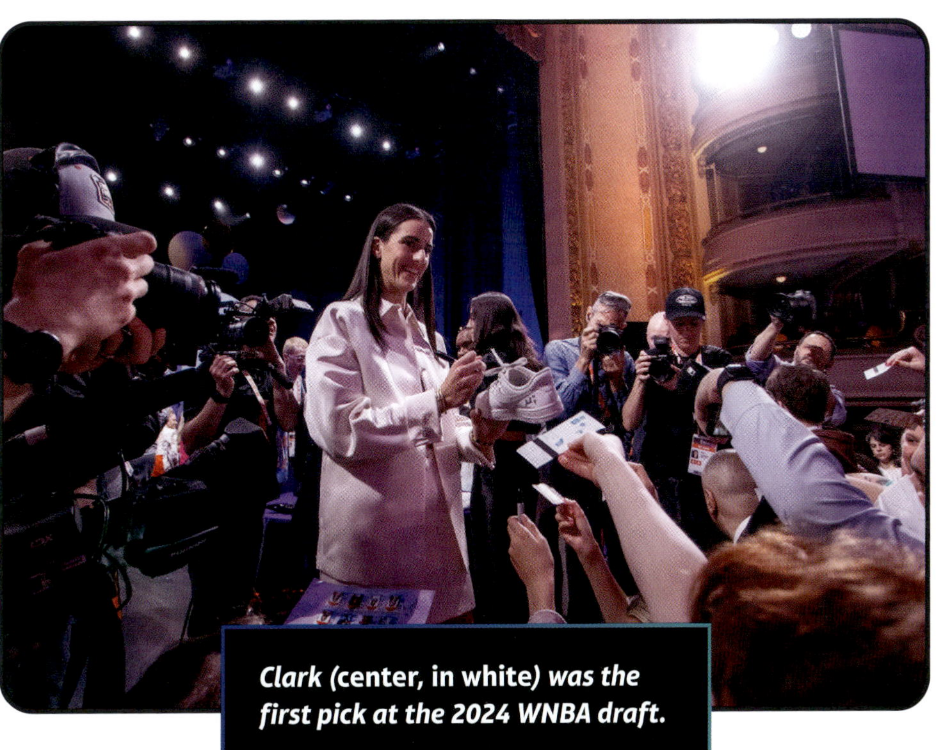

Clark (center, in white) *was the first pick at the 2024 WNBA draft.*

CHAPTER 2

Clark at a WNBA All-Star Game team practice in 2024

GAME CHANGERS

Miller and Clark both made fans more excited about women's basketball. They are both aggressive on the court. Miller loved athletic moves such as the jump shot and the crossover dribble. These were not common moves for female players in the 1980s.

In college, Miller helped the USC Trojans play a faster game that drew record crowds. Fans also liked her fun moves, such as wagging her wrist in the air after sinking long-range shots. Miller led the Trojans to two NCAA titles.

In 1983, Miller helped make NCAA history. She was part of the first all-Black starting lineup to win the women's title. These five players included twin sisters and forwards Pamela and Paula McGee. Miller had chosen USC in part so she could join these powerful players.

Miller (front row, third from right) *and her USC teammates celebrating their 1984 NCAA Championship win in Los Angeles, California, on April 1, 1984*

CONSIDER THIS

Miller worked for seventeen years as a TV sports analyst. In 1996, she became the first female sports analyst to announce plays for an NBA game on national TV.

After graduation, Miller became a women's basketball coach. She coached the USC Trojans from 1993 to 1995. Miller also worked as a TV sports analyst. She later returned to coaching college basketball. She even coached one of the 2024 WNBA All-Star teams. Clark was one of the players.

Miller found success as a coach after her playing career ended.

Like Miller, Caitlin Clark grew up playing sports with her brothers. She wanted to win every sport or board game she played. Caitlin played basketball with older girls and boys. This helped her build skills faster. At Iowa, she made longer three-point shots because of her training.

Clark (left) launches the ball over an Ohio State player during a game on January 21, 2024.

Fans loved these long shots. In March 2024, a record 3.4 million TV viewers watched Iowa play Ohio State. They wanted to see if Clark would break the NCAA Division I career scoring record. After missing a three-pointer, she hit two free throws to break the record.

Iowa played South Carolina in the 2024 NCAA women's basketball championship game. For the first time in history, more viewers watched this game than the men's championship. Although Iowa lost, Clark scored 30 points. She ended her NCAA career with an amazing record of 3,951 points.

CHAPTER 3

Miller (center) with teammates and her gold medal at the 1984 Summer Olympics

GOLD STARS

Miller and Clark were both stars on their school teams, and both played with the US national team. In high school, Miller scored a total of 3,446 points. This California record wasn't broken until 2023.

In college, Miller racked up 3,018 points while playing for USC. As of 2024, no Trojan player has broken this record.

In 1983 and 1984, Miller was named the NCAA's Most Outstanding Player. She also earned three Naismith Awards at USC. This award is named after Dr. James Naismith, who created basketball in 1891. It honors top players in college basketball.

Miller at the Basketball Hall of Fame in September 2012

Miller (front row, center) and teammates lift head coach Pat Summitt as they celebrate their gold medal win over South Korea at the 1984 Summer Olympics.

Miller also played for Team USA while she was attending USC. In 1983, she helped the US Women's National Basketball Team win a gold medal at the Pan American Games in Venezuela. The next year, she helped the US team win its first Olympic gold medal at the Summer Olympics in Los Angeles, California. After graduating from USC, Miller earned a third gold medal. This time, she helped the United States beat the former Soviet Union at the 1986 Goodwill Games.

CONSIDER THIS

In 2006, USC honored Cheryl Miller by retiring her Trojans jersey number. This means no other USC women's basketball player can wear Miller's number 31.

Clark racked up 2,547 points while playing for Dowling Catholic High. In college, Clark scored over 1,000 points in each of her last two years in Iowa. She won the Nancy Lieberman award both years. Nancy Lieberman was a star guard who played in the 1970s and 1980s. The award named after her honors the top point guard of the year in women's NCAA Division I basketball. Clark also won Naismith Awards in 2023 and 2024.

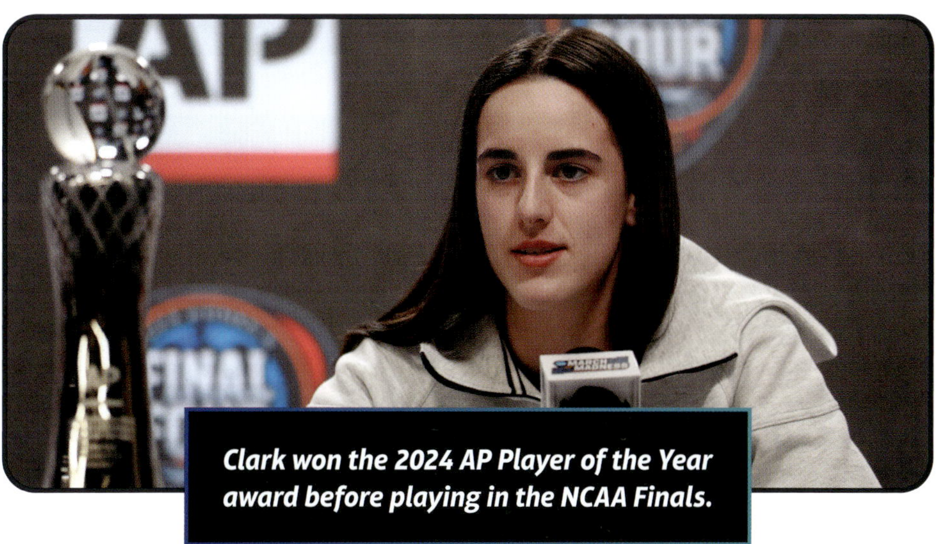

Clark won the 2024 AP Player of the Year award before playing in the NCAA Finals.

Clark played on US women's junior teams to win three gold medals in 2017, 2019, and 2021. She was named to the US National Women's Team in April 2024. That same year, she was named Player of the Year by ESPN.

Some fans were upset Clark was not a member of the 2024 Olympic Women's Basketball Team that won gold in Paris, France. But Clark was named to the 2024 WNBA All-Star team. Clark and other WNBA All-Stars and the Olympic team played a game to help the US prepare for the Olympics. Miller was the team coach. Clark called the Olympics a dream to work toward in the future.

Clark (right) with Kelsey Plum of the Las Vegas Aces on July 2, 2024

Clark (left), playing for the Indiana Fever, attempts to block a play by Diana Taurasi of the Phoenix Mercury on June 30, 2024.

CHAPTER 4

Miller was known for her aggressive style of play.

AND THE WINNER IS

It can be hard to compare athletes who played at different times because the sports world is always changing. For example, Clark is famous for her deep three-point shots. But Miller played before the NCAA added the three-point line to women's basketball in 1987. In 2024, Clark started breaking records in the WNBA. But Miller played before the WNBA began in 1997.

With Clark in the spotlight in recent years, fans and sports analysts have been debating whether she is better than past players like Miller. Clark fans can point to her NCAA records and her strong start in the WNBA. In July 2024, she became the first WNBA rookie to score a triple-double. This means she had double digits in three stats in one game. She finished the game with 19 points, 12 rebounds, and 13 assists.

Clark handles the ball while playing against the New York Liberty in 2024.

Miller fans can point to her two NCAA titles and her Olympic gold medal. She also paved the way for future female players with her athletic style of play. Miller helped promote the WNBA. She was one of the league's first coaches. She led the Phoenix Mercury to the 1998 WNBA Finals. In 1999, Miller was named to the Naismith Basketball Hall of Fame.

Miller's amazing career makes her the winner of this smackdown—for now. But Clark is still playing and setting more records. Both Miller and Clark are basketball legends. When choosing a winner, there is no right or wrong answer. People have different opinions about what makes a basketball player great. Who do you think is best? Think about their stories and make your own choice!

Clark smiles after her first WNBA triple-double in July 2024.

Miller, head coach of Team WNBA, at a WNBA All-Star Game team practice in July 2024

SMACKDOWN BREAKDOWN

CHERYL MILLER

Date of birth: January 3, 1964
Height: 6 feet 2 (1.9 m)
Total NCAA points: 3,018
NCAA championships: 2
Naismith Awards: 3

Stats are accurate through the 2023–2024 NCAA regular season.

CAITLIN CLARK

Date of birth: January 22, 2002
Height: 6 feet (1.8 m)
Total NCAA points: 3,951
NCAA championships: 0
Naismith Awards: 2

GLOSSARY

assist: a pass from a teammate that leads directly to a basket

crossover: when a dribbling player switches the basketball from one hand to the other while changing direction

Division I: the highest level of competition for college athletes in the US

draft: when teams take turns choosing new players

dribble: when a player bounces a basketball while moving around the court

free throw: an open shot taken from behind a set line after a foul by an opponent

jump shot: when a player shoots the basketball while jumping

NCAA: National Collegiate Athletic Association; the group that oversees college sports in the US

rebound: grabbing and controlling the ball after a missed shot

rookie: a first-year player

sharpshooter: one skilled at shooting

sports analyst: someone who provides information about plays and players during a game

LEARN MORE

Britannica Kids: Caitlin Clark
https://kids.britannica.com/students/article/Caitlin-Clark/641778

Britannica Kids: Cheryl Miller
https://kids.britannica.com/students/article/Miller-Cheryl/312509

Goldstein, Margaret J. *Meet Caitlin Clark: Basketball Superstar.* Minneapolis: Lerner Publications, 2025.

Hewson, Anthony K. *Caitlin Clark*. Mendota Heights, MN: Press Box Books, 2024.

Lowe, Alexander. *G.O.A.T. Basketball Point Guards*. Minneapolis: Lerner Publications, 2023.

WNBA: Caitlin Clark
https://www.wnba.com/player/1642286/caitlin-clark

INDEX

PHOTO ACKNOWLEDGMENTS

Image credits: Peter Read Miller/Sports Illustrated via Getty Images, pp. 4, 8, 10, 15, 18; G Fiume/Getty Images, pp. 5, 29; David Berding/Getty Images, p. 6; Kirk Irwin/Getty Images, pp. 7, 17; Jim Rogash/Getty Images, pp. 9, 19; Marc Piscotty/Icon Sportswire via Getty Images, p. 11; Luke Lu/Diamond Images via Getty Images, p. 12; Cora Veltman/Sportico via Getty Images, p. 13; Alex Slitz/Getty Images, pp. 14, 27; Brian Bahr/Allsport via Getty Images, p. 16; Jayne Kamin-Oncea/Getty Images, p. 20; Gregory Shamus/Getty Images, p. 21; Ethan Miller/Getty Images, p. 22; Chris Coduto/Getty Images, p. 23; Rick Stewart/Getty Images, p. 24; Michael Hickey/Getty Images, pp. 25, 26; David Madison/Getty Images, p. 28.

Cover: AP Photo/Ashley Landis (Clark); Tony Duffy/Getty Images (Miller).